D0427088

	DATE DUE		
APR 4 '00			
APR 26 '00			
AUG 04 '00			
NOV 6 02			
APR 22 '03			
AUG 6 '03			
JUL 11 '05			
APR 14 '08			
JUL 29 '09			

GREAT BOOK OF RIDDLES & JOKES

Joseph Rosenbloom
Illustrated by
Sanford Hoffman

Sterling Publishing Co., Inc.
New York

To Sheila Barry

10   9   8   7   6   5   4   3   2   1

Published by Sterling Publishing Company, Inc.
387 Park Avenue South, New York, NY 10016
Excerpted from *Giggles, Gags & Groaners*
© 1987 by Joseph Rosenbloom
Distributed in Canada by Sterling Publishing
% Canadian Manda Group, One Atlantic Avenue, Suite 105
Toronto, Ontario, Canada M6K 3E7
Distributed in Great Britain and Europe by Chris Lloyd
463 Ashley Road, Parkstone, Poole, Dorset, BH14 0AX, England
Distributed in Australia by Capricorn Link (Australia) Pty Ltd.
P.O. Box 6651, Baulkham Hills, Business Centre, NSW 2153, Australia
Manufactured in the United States of America

Sterling ISBN 0-8069-9834-2

Contents

Books by Joseph Rosenbloom

1.
QUICK QUIPS

If a fly and a flea pass each other, what time is it?
Fly past flea.

What is wrinkled, masked and rides a horse?
The Lone Prune.

Why do elephants have wrinkled ankles?
They tie their sneakers too tight.

Did you hear the joke about the hole in the ground?
Never mind. You wouldn't dig it.

Did you hear the joke about the eraser?
Never mind. It would rub you the wrong way.

What is soft and cuddly and goes "Oink, oink"?
A teddy boar.

Why do elephants want to be alone?
Because two's a crowd.

NIT: Somebody robbed the bakery yesterday.
WIT: Doesn't that take the cake!

NIT: The racing driver was really depressed.
WIT: Isn't that the pits!

NIT: I've forgotten everything I ever learned.
WIT: Well, what do you know?

What goes, "Tick-tick, woof-woof"?
A watch dog.

"Is your watch dog any good?"

"Oh, yes. If you hear a suspicious noise in the middle of the night, just wake him up and he'll bark."

Why does a dog sit on its hind legs?
If it didn't, it would be standing up.

What does a dog do that a man steps into?
Pants.

WOMAN: Can I have a puppy for my son?
PET SHOP OWNER: Sorry, ma'am, we don't swap.

MAN: Have you any dogs going cheap?
PET STORE OWNER: No, sir, all our dogs go "Woof."

What is the difference between a flea-bitten dog and a bored student?
One is going to itch, the other is itching to go.

What is the difference between a good dog and a bad student?
One rarely bites, the other barely writes.

What is the difference between a fly and a bird?
A bird can fly, but a fly can't bird.

Sign outside school:

FITE ILLETERACY (*Fight Illiteracy*)

Why was the letter "E" left back?
Because it was always in bed and never in school.

What starts with an *e* and ends with an *e*, but has only one letter in it?
An envelope.

Did you hear about the romance in the post office?
A stamp was stuck on an envelope.

What is the difference between a cover girl and a postage stamp?
One is a female, the other is a mail fee.

What did one gust of smoke say to another gust of smoke as it went up the chimney?
"I'm going out—can I borrow your soot (suit)?"

What did the hamburger say to the ketchup bottle?
"That's enough out of you."

How do you talk to a cobra?
Poison-to-poison.

What is yellow and goes, "Ho-ho-ho"?
Santa Banana.

What is yellow and goes "Phut - phut - phut?"
An outboard lemon.

What is yellow, stands in a river during a storm and doesn't get wet?
A canary with an umbrella.

What would you get if you crossed a duck with a dog?
A duckshund (dachshund).

What is brown and greasy and stays in a tower?
The lunch bag of Notre Dame.

Who went into the lion's den and came out alive?
The lion.

Where does a skunk sit in church?
In a pew.

Did you hear the joke about the giraffe?
Never mind. It's way over your head.

Did you hear the joke about the sandwich?
Never mind. It's a lot of baloney.

What is the first thing a gorilla learns in school?
The Ape-B-C's.

How many hairs are there on a pig's head?
The next time you use a comb, count them.

How many ribs are there on a jackass?
Open your shirt and you'll find out.

How many toes does a monkey have?
Take off your shoes and let's look.

Why don't monkeys live on the moon?
Because there are no bananas there.

What do Alexander the Great and Smokey the Bear have in common?
The same middle name.

What buzzed around King Arthur's head?
The Gnats (Knights) of the Round Table.

What is a pirate's favorite pet?
A cat-o'-nine-tails.

What is a cat's favorite nursery rhyme?
"Three Blind Mice."

What do you get if your cat swallows a parrot?
A purr-a-keet (parakeet).

Why did little Audrey wear only one boot?
Because she heard that the snow was one foot deep.

What time is it when four men are shovelling snow with a policeman watching them?
Wintertime.

Why does it snow in the winter?
Because snow would melt in the summer.

How is a winter day different from an unconscious boxer?
One is cold out, the other is out cold.

What goes up when you count down?
A rocket.

What did the zombie child call his father?
"Deady."

2.
SILLIES
@ DILLIES

"Doctor, doctor, people keep making fun of me."
"Get out of here, you silly fool!"

What is worse than being with a fool?
Fooling with a bee.

Which Muppet is hard to see through?
Kermit the Fog.

What did the yodeller say when he got thrown out
of the boarding house for nonpayment of rent?
He said, "That's what happens when you owe
the old lady" (yoh-de-oh-lay-dee).

BOY SCOUT: How much after midnight is it?
TENDERFOOT: I don't know. My watch only goes
as high as twelve.

What do misers do when it is cold?
They sit around a candle.

What do misers do when it is *very* cold?
They light it.

CUSTOMER: I want my moncy back.
CLERK: What's the problem?
CUSTOMER: I bought some birdseed here and it was no good.
CLERK: Wouldn't the birds eat it?
CUSTOMER: *What* birds? I planted every one of those seeds and not even a single bird came up!

An absent-minded professor came home late one night. When he reached his door, he realized he had forgotten his key. He knocked and knocked until finally his wife peeked out the door. Since it was very dark, she didn't recognize him. "I'm sorry, sir," she said, "but the professor isn't home."

The professor, absent-minded as usual, replied, "Okay, I'll come back tomorrow."

ONE OF THE WORLD'S SILLIEST CHILD ABUSE JOKES

Looking through a window, a man saw a woman hitting a boy over the head with a loaf of bread. Deciding it was none of his business, the man walked on. But he passed the house every day and he saw the same thing the next day, and the day after that. Every morning for six months the lady hit the boy on the head with a loaf of bread.

Then, one morning, the woman threw a chocolate cake into the boy's face. Astonished, the man poked his head in the window and asked why.

"Oh," the woman replied, "Today is his birthday."

Sign in front of clock repair shop:

```
CUCKOO  CLOCKS
PSYCHOANALYZED  CHEAP
```

Why do rats have long tails?
They can't remember short stories.

What has sharp teeth, chops down cherry trees
and founded a country?
Jaws Washington.

Visiting an observatory, the hillbilly watched the
astronomer look through his telescope.

Just then a star fell.

"Wow—ee!" said the hillbilly. "Are you a great
shot!"

Little Audrey was taken to the museum by her
father. One room they came to was filled with
modern paintings, and a sign on the wall read,
"Art Objects." Turning to her father, little Audrey
said, "If Art objects, why is he letting them show
his paintings?"

NIT: Have you ever seen an oil well?
WIT: No, but I've never seen one sick either.

SNAKE CHARMER: Be careful with that case! It contains a ten-foot snake.

PORTER: You can't kid me. Snakes don't have feet.

An old lady, who lived on the third floor of a boardinghouse, broke her leg. As the doctor put a cast on it, he warned her not to climb any stairs.

Several months later, the doctor took off the cast.

"Can I climb stairs now?" asked the little old lady.

"Yes," he replied.

"Thank goodness!" she said. "I'm sick and tired of shinnying up and down that drainpipe!"

"Doctor, I keep thinking I'm a horse."

"Well, I can cure you, but it's going to cost you a lot of money."

"Money's no problem. I just won the Kentucky Derby."

Did you hear about the two stupid bear hunters? When they came to a sign that said BEAR LEFT they went home.

Why did Little Audrey take all her clothes off in the laundromat?

Because the sign on the washing machine said: "When The Machine Stops, Remove Your Clothes."

FREDDY: I see your new microscope magnifies three times.

TEDDY: Oh, no! And I've used it twice already!

"I've come to ask for your daughter's hand."

"I can't allow that. Either you take my whole daughter, or nothing."

Lem and Clem stood by a car in which they had locked the key.

"Why don't we get a coat hanger to open it?" Lem asked.

"No," answered Clem. "People will think we're trying to break in."

Lem said, "What if we use a pocket knife to cut around the rubber, then stick a finger in and pull up the lock?"

"No," said Clem. "People will think we're too dumb to use a coat hanger.

"Well," sighed Lem, "we'd better think of something fast. It's starting to rain and the sun roof is open!"

"My mother is so fussy . . ."

"How fussy is she?"

"My mother is so fussy that last night at 2 A.M. I went to the kitchen to get a glass of water and when I got back—my bed was made!"

A man who had always wanted a parrot saw a pet shop with the sign: GOING OUT OF BUSINESS AUCTION. Here, he thought, was his chance to get a parrot cheap. He went into the shop and there, sure enough, was a magnificent-looking parrot.

When the parrot was put up for sale, however, the bidding went higher and higher. Finally, the parrot was his!

The man left the store delighted with his purchase, but soon he had second thoughts. He had paid a lot of money for the bird. What if it wouldn't talk?

Back he went to the pet shop and demanded of the auctioneer, "Say, does this parrot talk? If it doesn't, I want my money back!"

Upon hearing this, the parrot spoke: "Not talk! Who do you think was bidding against you in the auction?"

You're temperamental: 50% temper, 50% mental.

3. LAW & DISORDER

What did the judge say when the skunk came into the courtroom?

"Odor in the court!"

JUDGE: You have a choice: 30 days or a hundred dollars.

DEFENDANT: I'll take the money.

Who is the biggest gangster in the sea?

Al Ca-prawn.

What's wrinkled, purple, and carries a machine gun?

Al Ca-prune.

What kind of ship do the police have to keep an eye on?

A thug boat.

NIT: I'm never going to gamble again.

WIT: I don't believe you. You'll never quit gambling.

NIT: Want to bet?

A father wanted to cure his son of gambling. He asked the boy's principal for help.

The next day the principal called the boy's father. "I think I have cured your son of gambling," he said.

"How did you do it?" asked the father.

"Well, he looked at my beard and said, 'Sir, is that beard real or false? I wouldn't mind betting $5 that it is false.' 'All right,' I replied. 'I'll take your bet. Now pull it and see.' Of course, my beard is real," said the principal. "He had to pay me $5. So I'm sure that will cure him of gambling."

"Oh, no!" groaned the father. "Last night he bet me $10 you'd let him pull your beard!"

Sign in store window:

DON'T BE FOOLED BY IMITATORS GOING OUT OF BUSINESS. WE HAVE BEEN GOING OUT OF BUSINESS LONGER THAN ANYONE IN TOWN.

Another sign in the store window:

DON'T GO ANYWHERE ELSE AND BE ROBBED—TRY US!

How do you get nuts from a squirrel?
You walk up to the squirrel and say, "This is a stick-up!"

Why was the lamb punished?
Because it was baaaa-d.

What happened to the very bad egg?
It was eggs-secuted.

What did the egg say to the blender?
"I know when I'm beaten."

What is yellow and goes round and round?
A banana in a washing machine.

MASKED MAN: Here's one thousand dollars.

POOR MAN: What's this for?

MASKED MAN: I steal from the rich and give to the poor.

POOR MAN: Wow? I'm rich!

MASKED MAN: All right—stick 'em up!

Why did the cucumber need a lawyer?
Because it was in a pickle.

Why did the strawberry need a lawyer?
Because it was in a jam.

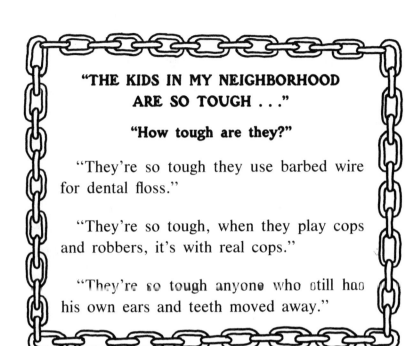

"THE KIDS IN MY NEIGHBORHOOD ARE SO TOUGH . . ."

"How tough are they?"

"They're so tough they use barbed wire for dental floss."

"They're so tough, when they play cops and robbers, it's with real cops."

"They're so tough anyone who still has his own ears and teeth moved away."

Did you hear about the gangsters who jumped out of an airplane? They had a chute out.

What do you call a bird gangster?
Robin Hood.

What do you give someone who has everything?
A burglar alarm.

WIFE: Harry, are you awake? There's a burglar downstairs.
HARRY: No, I'm asleep.

"How long are you in for?"

"Ninety-nine years. How long are you in for?"

"Seventy-five."

"Okay, you take the cot by the door. You'll be getting out first."

BOOKS FOR THE PRISON LIBRARY

The Gangsters by Robin Steele
My Life in Crime by Upton O. Goode
Bad Money by Count R. Fitz
You Always Get Caught by Sue Nora Later

JAILER (*hearing hacksaw sounds*): What are you doing?

PRISONER: I have to confess. I'm sawing the bars.

JAILER: Where's your grammar? You should say, "I'm seeing the bars."

Two prisoners were about to face the firing squad.

"Have you one last request?"

"Yes," began the first, "I . . ."

"Shh," interrupted the second. "Don't make trouble."

To whom should you go for help when you're attacked by killer flies?

The SWAT Team.

DIT: What were Tarzan's last words?
DOT: Who greased the grapevine?
DIT: Well, who did?
DOT: Oh, some grease monkey.

What starts out battered and ends up flattened?

A pancake.

What is grey and goes around stamping out forest fires?

Smokey the Elephant.

A policeman in a patrol car was astonished to see a woman knitting while driving her car.

He drove up alongside her and called, "Pull over!"

"No," she called back, "a pair of socks!"

MRS. SMITH: I got a ticket yesterday, and I was only going five miles an hour.

MRS. JONES: I find that hard to believe. Where were you driving?

MRS. SMITH: Right here in town. I was so upset I almost drove right off the sidewalk.

What did Achilles say as he lay dying after being wounded in the heel?

"My feet are killing me!"

Sign on newly-mown lawn:

> YOUR FEET ARE KILLING ME

WATSON: What is your favorite tree, Holmes?

HOLMES: A lemon tree (*elementary*), my dear Watson.

4. YUCK!

A dog walked into a fast-food restaurant and ordered a thick shake. He drank it without fuss or delay and left.

The customers in the restaurant were amazed. One of them said to the clerk behind the counter, "That's quite a dog! Does he always do that?"

"Oh, no," the clerk answered calmly. "He usually orders a large coke."

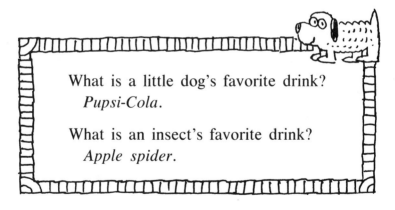

What is a little dog's favorite drink?
Pupsi-Cola.

What is an insect's favorite drink?
Apple spider.

Did you hear the story about the coffee?
Never mind. It's hot stuff.

On what day do people drink the most water?
Thirst-day.

Sign in front of ice cream store:

What cake wanted to rule the world?
Attila the Bun.

In a restaurant you must choose between eating an
elephant egg or a five-hundred pound canary egg.
Which would you pick?
*A five-hundred pound canary egg, because
everyone hates elephant yolks.*

What is thin, romantic and greasy?
Chips that pass in the night.

What did the cow say when it had nothing to eat
but a thistle?
"Thistle have to do."

What is grey and powdery?
Instant elephant.

What weighs two thousand pounds and is covered
with lettuce and special sauce?
A Big McElephant.

What do cats like on their hot dogs?
Mouse-tard.

Can mustard be friendly with a hot dog bun?
Yes, if they have a frank relationship.

Where do extra-smart frankfurters end up?
On honor rolls.

CUSTOMER: Make me a hamburger!
WAITER: Okay—poof! You're a hamburger!

Why couldn't the hamburger speak?
Because the catsup got its tongue.

Who was the burger's all-time favorite movie director?

Sizzle B. DeMille.

What do frogs eat
with their hamburgers?
French flies.

A man was eating a hamburger in the park. Next to him sat a lady with a small dog. The dog smelled the man's food and began whining and jumping up at him.

"Do you mind if I throw him a bit?" asked the man.

"Not at all," said the lady, pleased.

So the man picked up the dog and threw it over the wall.

How do you make a cream puff?
Chase it around the block.

Do you know what Mary had when she went out to dinner?
Everybody knows Mary had a little lamb.

What is yellow and white and goes 600 miles per hour?
A pilot's egg sandwich.

What is convenient and weighs 20,000 pounds?
An elephant six-pack.

What is the difference between an Indian and an African elephant?
About three thousand miles.

What is white and fluffy and swings from cake to cake?
A meringue-utang (orangutan).

What is the difference between a moldy vegetable and a depressing song?
One is a bad salad, the other a sad ballad.

What do you get if you cross an egg and a soda?
Yolka-Cola.

ONE OF THE WORLD'S SILLIEST GOLDFISH JOKES

A newspaper columnist who wrote about money received a phone call from a stranger who spoke in an unusually low voice.

"I do not agree with you about the high cost of living," the voice said. "I'll have you know that my wife and I eat to our hearts' content for exactly 42 cents a week."

"Forty-two cents a week!" exclaimed the columnist, "I find that hard to believe. How do you do it?"

A burst of static came over the telephone line.

"What's that?" said the columnist. "Please speak louder."

"I can't speak louder," said the voice. "I'm a goldfish."

What do whales like to chew?
Blubber gum.

How does a lion like his steak?
Medium roar (rare).

Did you hear the joke about the rotten food?
Never mind. It turns my stomach.

Did you hear the joke about the rotten pudding?
Never mind. You wouldn't swallow it.

Did you hear the joke about the man who swallowed a bone?
Never mind. It chokes me up.

A squirrel who lived in the zoo was leaning against a sign that read, DO NOT FEED THE BEARS. A hand-lettered notice around the squirrel's neck read, PLEASE FEED ME. I'M NOT A BEAR.

What kind of snack do little monkeys have with their milk?
Chocolate chimp cookies.

What is a lemming's favorite dessert?
Lemming (lemon) meringue pie.

"Mother, may I leave the table?"
"Well, you certainly can't take it with you!"

What do you get when you cross a pig and a centipede?

Bacon and legs.

What do you get when you cross a dog and a chicken?

Barkin' and eggs.

What do you get when you cross a lighthouse and a chicken coop?

Beacon and eggs.

What is a cat's favorite breakfast?

Mice Krispies.

What is golden brown, flat, has maple syrup on it, and doesn't want to grow up?

Peter Pancake.

BOOKS FOR COOKS

Italian Food by Liz Anya, Manny Kotty,
   Minnie Stroni and Lynn Guini
The Tin Can Cookbook by Billie Gote
Stomach Cramps by Henrietta Greenapple
Time to Eat! by Dean R. Bell

CUSTOMER: Why is this bread full of holes?
BAKER: It's whole-wheat bread.

How do they tell that there's bread in the bakery?
They have a roll call.

Did you hear the joke about the one-week-old bread?
Never mind, it's too stale.

What has bread on both sides and frightens easily?
A chicken sandwich.

What kind of sandwiches do cows like?
Bull-only (bologna) sandwiches.

How do you keep peanut butter from sticking to the roof of your mouth?
Turn the bread upside down.

What flies and wobbles?
A jelly-copter.

Why did the jelly wobble?
It saw the milk shake.

What made the biscuit box?
It saw the fruit punch.

What is long and skinny and short and round?
Spaghetti and meatballs.

THE WORLD'S WORST PIZZA JOKE

Once there was an ogre named Pete who had the Evil Eye. He could take one look at you and zap you. Everyone around town was afraid of Pete's Zap Eye (pizza pie).

What's the difference between a stupid person and a pizza?
One is easy to cheat, the other is cheesy to eat.

What is red and white on the outside and grey and lumpy on the inside?
A can of Cream of Elephant soup.

What is red, has bumps and lives in the West?
The Lone Raspberry.

What fruit rides in an ambulance?
A pear-amedic (paramedic).

When is a Chinese restaurant successful?
When it makes a fortune, cookie.

CUSTOMER: Waiter, you've got your thumb on my steak!
WAITER: Well, I didn't want it to fall on the floor again.

CUSTOMER: Waiter, there's a fly in my soup!
WAITER: It's the rotting meat that attracts them.

CUSTOMER: Waiter, your tie is in my soup!
WAITER: That's all right, sir. It won't shrink.

CUSTOMER: Waiter, there a fly in my soup!
WAITER: No, sir, that's the last customer. The chef's a witch doctor.

CUSTOMER: Waiter, there's a fly in my soup!"
WAITER: Yes, sir. And if you push over that pea, he'll play water polo.

A frog went into a restaurant and ordered soup. When it was served, the frog turned to the waiter and complained, "Waiter, there's no fly in my soup!"

5.
ALL WET!

How do you keep from getting wet when you're in the shower?
Don't turn the water on.

What is grey and wet and lives in Florida?
A melted penguin.

Which animal goes, "Cluck, bubble, cluck, bubble, cluck, bubble?"
A chicken of the sea.

What has four eyes and is very wet?
The Mississippi.

What lives under water and goes, "Dit-dot-dit-dot-dot-dit?"
A Morse cod.

A FISHY STORY

"Are all the *fish* here today?"

"Now how *shad* I know? Am I my brother's *kipper*?"

"No, but I've been *herring* things about you."

"Yes, that's the *halibut*. But it's all a *fluke*."

"*Salmons* been talking about you. They said you *smelt* and were a real '*eel*."

"Did I *clam* I wasn't? Don't *carp* on it."
"I *octopus* your face in!"

"I'm not afraid of your *mussels*, *Squid*. Don't *snapper* at me. I'm not your *sole* problem."

"*Whale*, I'd better go. There's no *porpoise* in talking to you. You *shark* can ruin anyone's day."

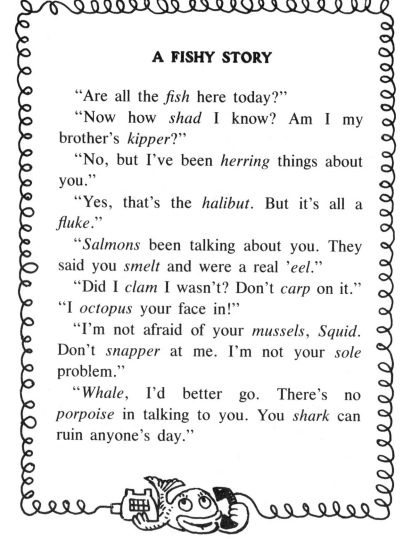

What would you have if you crossed the Pacific Ocean with a chili pepper?

Heat waves.

What happens when you have an argument with a shark?

You get chewed out.

What old-time comedian do sharks like?

Groucho Sharks (Marx).

What kind of fish has two knees?
A tunee fish.

What fish goes shopping and drives a Porsche?
A yuppie guppy.

What two fish are needed to make a shoe?
A sole and an 'eel.

What wears cowboy boots, holds two guns and lives under water?
Billy the Squid.

What do you call a swimmer at the scene of a crime?
An eye wetness.

LITTLE AUDREY: How many fish have you caught, sir?

FISHERMAN: None yet. But I've only been fishing for an hour.

LITTLE AUDREY: You're doing better than the man who was here yesterday.

FISHERMAN: Really? How am I doing better?

LITTLE AUDREY: It took him five hours to do what you just did in one hour.

FISH WARDEN: That sign says, "No Fishing Allowed."

LITTLE BOY: It's okay, I'm fishing silently.

What fish are other fish afraid of?
Jack the Kipper.

"For a quarter I'll imitate a fish," said the little boy.

"And how will you do that, my little man?" asked a lady. "Swim?"

"None of those cheap imitations," said the little boy. "I'll eat a worm."

Why do teakettles whistle?
Because they never learned to sing.

Once upon a time there was a fisherman who was always talking about the giant fish he almost caught. One day he took his two sons, Toward and Away, fishing with him.

That night he returned more excited than ever.

"Honey," he yelled to his wife. "You should have seen the fish I saw today! A tremendous green fish, ten feet long with horns and fur all over its back. It came crawling out of the water, snatched our son Toward, and swallowed him in one gulp!"

"Good gracious!" exclaimed his wife. "That's horrible!"

"Oh, that was nothing," said her husband. "You should have seen the one that got Away!"

Did you hear the story about the water bucket with holes in it?
Never mind. I don't want it to leak out.

Did you hear the joke about the ocean?
Never mind. It's too deep for you.

Sign on dentist's houseboat:

OFFSHORE DRILLING

What is a mermaid?
A deep-she fish.

What do mermaids like for breakfast?
Merma-lade on toast.

LEM: How's the fishing around here?

CLEM: It's fine.

LEM: Then how come you haven't caught any fish?

CLEM: You asked me about fishing, not catching.

What children live in the ocean?
Buoys and gulls.

How do the oceans cook?
By microwave.

What is the difference between land and sea?
The land is dirt-y and the sea is tide-y.

What is the difference between a sailor and a bargain hunter?
One sails the seas, the other sees the sales.

NUTTY NONSENSE LIMERICK

A ghoul stood on the bridge one night,
Its lips were all a-quiver.
It gave a cough,
Its leg fell off
And floated down the river.

TED: My cabin on the ship was nice, but that washing machine on the wall was terrible.
ALICE: Washing machine? That was the porthole!
TED: No wonder I never got my clothes back!

What sits on the bottom of the sea and makes you an offer you can't refuse?

The Cod Father.

What sits on the bottom of the sea and is made of chocolate?

An oyster egg.

What do you get from an educated oyster?

Pearls of wisdom.

Sign in fish store window:

BOY WANTED TO OPEN OYSTERS ABOUT
16 YEARS OLD

SHAGGY DOG STORY

Two men were walking along the beach with a small shaggy dog. The dog's owner threw a stick into the sea. The dog immediately dashed after the stick by running on top of the water. He brought the stick back to his master.

The other man couldn't believe his eyes. "That is a very remarkable dog you have there," he said.

"Remarkable, my foot!" said the dog's owner. "After all the lessons he's had, he still won't learn to swim!"

Four-year-old Suzi, visiting her aunt's summer cottage, was watching a couple of water skiers on the lake. Turning to her aunt, she said, "Those men are so dumb. They're never going to catch up with that boat."

6.
TOTALLY
SICK

Where do you take sick kangaroos?
To the hop-ital.

How do you take a sick pig to the hospital?
In the ham-bulance.

Where do you take sick dogs?
To the dog-tor.

Where do they send homeless dogs?
To the arph-anage (orphanage).

PATIENT: Doctor, doctor! I feel like a dog!
DOCTOR: Don't worry, but please get down off the couch.

PATIENT: Doctor, doctor, I feel like a dog!
DOCTOR: Sit!

PATIENT: Doctor, doctor! I think I'm a bird.

DOCTOR: Well, don't get in a flap. Just perch on a chair.

"Doctor, doctor! Last night I heard a ringing in my ears!"

"Well, where did you expect to hear it?"

DOCTOR: I have some good news and some bad news.

PATIENT: Tell me the bad news first.

DOCTOR: You have canary disease.

PATIENT: What's the good news?

DOCTOR: It's tweetable.

DOCTOR: I have some bad news and even worse news. The bad news is that you have only 24 hours to live.

PATIENT: Twenty-four hours to live! What worse news could there be?

DOCTOR: I should have told you the bad news yesterday.

PATIENT: During my operation, Nurse, I heard the surgeon use a four-letter word that upset me very much.

NURSE: What word was that?

PATIENT: "Oops!"

BABY SNAKE: Mommy, my head hurts!
MOMMY SNAKE: Come here, let me hiss it.

"My dog's head is always hanging down, so I'm taking him to the doctor."

"Neck's weak?"

"No, tomorrow."

What quacks and runs his country with an iron fist?

A duck-tator. (dictator).

"I knew someone who thinks he's an owl."
"Who?"
"Make that two people."

What do ants take when they are sick?
Antibiotics.

What do elephants take when they get hysterical?
Trunquilizers.

What did the baby computer say when it got hurt?
"I want my da-ta!"

What is a computer's first sign of old age?
Loss of memory.

PSYCHIATRIST (to NURSE): Please just say we're very busy—not that it's a madhouse!

PATIENT: Doctor, can I sleep in my contact lenses?
DOCTOR: No, your feet would stick out.

"D-d-d-oc-oc-t-or, Do-oc-oc-oc-t-or, I-I ha-ha-ve trou-bbb-be-lle ss-ss-sp-eak-eak-in-g-g-g."
"Sorry, I wasn't listening. Would you mind repeating that?"

DOCTOR: I'm sorry I made you wait so long.
PATIENT: I don't mind the wait so much, but I did think you'd like to treat my illness in its early stages.

BOOKS FOR THE DOCTOR'S WAITING ROOM

How to Make a Tourniquet by Hank R. Schiff
Handling Your Emotions by Mel N. Collie
Calm Down by Ed. G. Nerfs
Knocking Your Funny Bone by Lord Howard Hertz

What is grey, carries flowers, and cheers you up when you get sick?

A Get-Wellephant.

A travelling salesman, passing through a small town, saw a decrepit-looking old man sitting in a rocking chair on the porch of one of the houses. For all his years, however, the old man seemed so contented and happy that the salesman couldn't resist talking to him.

"You look as if you don't have a care in the world," the salesman said. "What is your secret for a long, happy life?"

"Well," replied the old man, "I smoke six packs of cigarettes a day, I drink a quart of whiskey every day and I chew snuff. I never wash and I go out every night."

"That's fantastic!" exclaimed the salesman. "How old are you, anyway?"

"Twenty-five," was the reply.

The little boy kept sniffling on his sleeve.

"Haven't you got a handkerchief?" asked an old lady.

"Yes, I do," said the little boy, "but I don't think my mother would like me to lend it to strangers."

MOTHER: I'm so worried about my son. All he does is scratch himself and swing from a tree.

DOCTOR: Don't worry. He is perfectly normal— just going through a phase.

MOTHER: Oh, thank you, doctor! How much do I owe you?

DOCTOR: Thirty bananas.

PATIENT: I don't think the pills you gave me are helping.

DOCTOR: Have you been taking two on an empty stomach?

PATIENT: Well, I've tried, but they keep rolling off.

What is the difference between a sick chicken and seven days?

One is a weak one, the other is one week.

What is the difference between a sick cow and an angry crowd?

One moos badly, the other boos madly.

What is the difference between a person with a cold and a prizefighter?

One blows his nose, the other knows his blows.

What is the difference between a healthy rabbit and a sick joke?

One is a fit bunny, the other is a bit funny.

> "What kind of dog is that?
>   "That's a Chihuahua."
> "A what?"
>   "A Chihuahua, a Chihuahua."
> "God bless you!"

What do you say when the Statue of Liberty sneezes?
  "God bless America!"

How does Sherlock Holmes sneeze?
  "A-clue! A-clue!"

How does a train conductor sneeze?
  "A-choo! A-choo!

How does a tennis player sneeze?
  "A-tennis-shoe! A-tennis-shoe!"

What paper is most like a sneeze?
  A tissue!

What is red, white and blue and good to have when you want to sneeze?
  Hanky Doodle Dandy.

How is a sneezing elephant like a spy?
  They both have a code in the head.

PATIENT: Doctor, doctor! I feel like a pack of cards.

DOCTOR: Wait here. I'll deal with you later.

"Doctor, you've got to help me! I was just playing the harmonica and I swallowed it!"

"Lucky you weren't playing the piano."

DOCTOR: What seems to be the trouble?

PATIENT: I keep thinking no one can hear me.

DOCTOR: What seems to be the trouble?

PATIENT: Doctor, I have a problem. I keep thinking there are two of me.

DOCTOR: Say that again. And this time, don't both speak at once.

PATIENT: Doctor, doctor, I think I'm a bell.

DOCTOR: Take two aspirins and ring me in the morning.

"Doctor, doctor, I keep thinking I'm invisible!"

"Who said that?"

7.
PLAY IT
AGAIN, SAM!

What is big, grey and has horns?
An elephant marching band.

Which American march is heard in the jungle?
"Tarzan Stripes Forever."

What did Tarzan say when he saw the elephants coming?
"Here come the elephants!"

What is the difference between an elephant and a piece of paper?
You can't make a paper airplane out of an elephant.

How do elephants talk to each other?
By 'elephone.

What game do children in Arabia play?
Hide-and-Sheik.

What game do monster children play?
Hyde-and-Shriek.

What game do hogs play?
Pig-pong.

What wallows in mud and carries colored eggs?
The Easter Piggie.

What has fuzzy pink ears and writes?
A ballpoint bunny.

How do you paint a rabbit purple?
With purple hare spray.

Where do you find rabbits in Paris?
They're in the hutch, back of Notre Dame.

What do Yuppie rabbits want to be when they get out of business school?
Million-hares.

What is a sheep's favorite comic strip?
Mutton Jeff.

What do you get if you cross a small bear and a skunk?
Winnie the Pooh.

What do you get if you cross Hamlet and a grape?
A grape Dane.

What do you get if you cross a hurricane with a comedian?
Gales of laughter.

What do you get if you cross a comedian and a hangman?
A practical choker.

What has leaves but no bark, a jacket but no tie, a spine but no bones, and is good company?
A book.

In what book do ducks look up words?
A duck-tionary.

What would you get if you cross a book of nursery rhymes with an orange?
Tales of Mother Juice.

Why do elephants have cracks between their toes?
For carrying their library cards.

"What time does the library open?" the man on the phone asked.

"Nine A.M." came the reply. "And what's the idea of calling me at home in the middle of the night to ask a question like that?"

"Not until nine A.M.?" the man asked in a disappointed voice.

"No, not till nine A.M.!" the librarian said. "Why do you want to get in before nine A.M.?"

"Who said I wanted to get in?" the man sighed sadly. "I want to get out."

Why was the clock thrown out of the library?
Because it tocked too much.

Little Harold was practicing the violin in the living room while his father was trying to read in the den. The family dog was lying in the den, and as the screeching sounds of Little Harold's violin reached his ears, he began to howl loudly.

The father listened to the dog and the violin as long as he could. Then he jumped up, slammed his paper to the floor and yelled above the noise, "For pity's sake, can't you play something the dog doesn't know?"

"My brother has been practicing the violin for twenty years."

"He must be good by now."

"Not really. It was nineteen years before he realized you weren't supposed to blow it."

"I play checkers with my kangaroo."
"Does he ever win?"
"All the time. You should see him jump."

What is grey, has large wings, a long nose and gives money to elephants?
The Tusk Fairy.

"My watch needs a new band."
"I didn't even know it could sing."

How is a song like a locked door?
You need the right key for both.

What's long, skinny and beats a drum?
Yankee Noodle.

What's the difference between a drummer and a chef?
One makes the beat, the other bakes the meat.

What do you call five bottles of Coca-Cola and 7-Up?
A pop group.

What pop group gets clothes whiter?
The Bleach Boys.

What did the Beatles say when they saw the avalanche?

"Here come the Rolling Stones!"

What kind of music do you get when a stone falls in the water?

Plunk rock.

What elf was a famous rock star?

Elf S. Presley.

Sign in front of a record shop:

RECORDS FOR SALE, FOR SALE, FOR SALE. . . .

What musical instrument is found in the bathroom?

A tuba toothpaste.

What comes before a tuba?

A one-ba.

What is King Tut's favorite television show?

"Name That Tomb."

What color is a guitar?

Plink.

Sign outside music store:

GONE CHOPIN. BACH IN A MINUET.

An African chieftain flew to London for a visit. He was met at the airport by news reporters.

"Good morning, Chief," one of the newsmen said. "Did you have a smooth flight?"

The chieftain made a series of sounds—crackles, hisses, roars, whistles—and then added in perfect English, "Yes, pleasant enough indeed."

"And how long do you plan to remain in London?"

The chieftain began his reply with the same unusual noises and completed it in excellent English.

"Tell me," asked the reporter, "Where did you learn to speak such fine English?"

Again the chieftain repeated those strange sounds. "Shortwave radio," he said.

BOOKS FOR HOBBYISTS

Band Playing by Clara Nett
Jazz Music by Tenna Saxe
Cuddly Toys by Ted E. Behr
The Stars Tell It All by Horace Cope
Sculpting the Gods of Greece and Rome
    by Jove

Another sign:

OUT TO LUNCH. USUALLY BACH BY ONE. OFFENBACH SOONER.

"I'm going to watch *The Green Monster from the Red Swamp* on television tonight."

"Don't you mean *The Red Monster from the Green Swamp*?"

"It doesn't make any difference. I have a black-and-white set."

What is brown and lumpy and given to actors and actresses?
Academy A-warts.

What is beautiful, grey and wears glass slippers?
Cinderelephant.

What is the difference between Cinderella and a neat hairpiece?
One is a well-bred maid, the other is a well-made braid.

A film crew was on location deep in the desert. One day an old Indian went up to the director and said, "Tomorrow rain."

The next day it rained.

A week later, the Indian went up to the director and said, "Tomorrow storm."

The next day there was a hailstorm.

"This Indian is incredible," said the director. He told his secretary to hire the Indian to predict the weather.

However, after several successful predictions, the old Indian didn't show up for two weeks. Finally the director sent for him.

"I have to shoot a big scene tomorrow," said the director, "and I'm depending on you. What will the weather be like?"

The Indian shrugged his shoulders. "Don't know," he said. "Radio broken."

"I made a couple of pictures in Hollywood, but I had to stop."

"Why? What happened?"

"My camera broke."

Sign outside of planetarium:

CAST OF THOUSANDS—
EVERY ONE A STAR

"That last joke of yours was two-thirds of a pun."
"How's that?"
"P.U."

Lem and Clem were watching an old Lone Ranger film.

"I bet you $10 the Lone Ranger falls off his horse," said Lem.

"Don't be crazy," said Clem. "The Lone Ranger never falls off his horse."

"I bet he does."

"All right," said Clem, "I'll bet $10 he doesn't."

They sat watching the film a few more minutes in silence. Outlaws began shooting. The Lone Ranger's horse reared, and off he fell.

"There! I told you!" shouted Lem.

"Oh, all right," said Clem. "Here's your $10."

"No, I can't take it," said Lem. "I've got to be honest with you. I've seen this film before."

"So have I," Clem answered. "But I didn't think he'd be fool enough to fall off twice!"

8.

GOING NOWHERE

What goes "peckety-peck" and points north?
A magnetic chicken.

Why did the chicken cross the road?
To see a man lay bricks.

Why did the chicken cross the playground?
To get to the other slide.

Why did the turkey cross the road?
The chicken retired and moved to Florida.

Why didn't the elephant cross the street?
Because it saw the zebra crossing.

What kind of elephants live at the North Pole?
Cold ones.

Why do elephants have trunks?
Because they'd look silly carrying suitcases.

What is yellow outside, grey inside and very crowded?

A school bus full of elephants.

What do you get when you cross a watermelon and a school bus?

A watermelon that seats 45 people.

What do you get if you cross a cactus and a bicycle?

A flat tire.

What do you get if you go out stepping with a five-hundred-pound canary?

Stepped on.

Billboard on road:

BELT YOUR FAMILY
AND SAVE THEIR LIVES

What did one road say to the other road?
"Hi, way!"

What did the Wright Brothers say when they invented the airplane?
"It's the only way to fly."

Did you hear the joke about the airplane?
Never mind. It just took off.

Did you hear the joke about the express train?
Never mind. You just missed it.

LITTLE OLD LADY: Sonny, would you help me across the street?
BOY SCOUT: Sure, but wouldn't it be easier if I helped you right here?

LITTLE OLD LADY: Sonny, would you see me across the street?
BOY SCOUT: I don't know, I'll go have a look.

Sign in front of a garage:

MAY WE HAVE THE NEXT DENTS?

Where does a rat go when it's teeth hurt?
To a rodent-ist.

How do mice find their way on long trips?
With rod-ent maps.

PATIENT: Doctor, you've got to help me. I think
I'm a bridge.
DOCTOR: Why, whatever has come over you?
PATIENT: So far, two trucks and a bus.

Sign outside tailor shop:

DON'T STAND OUTSIDE AND FAINT
—COME INSIDE AND HAVE A FIT!

"Madame, your dog has been seen chasing a man on a bicycle."

"Nonsense, officer. My dog doesn't know how to ride a bicycle."

Why did the dog have to go to court?
He got a barking ticket.

What is a dog's favorite motorcycle?
A Hounda.

What kind of shot makes cars go?
A fuel injection.

Did you ever wonder why people park their cars in driveways and drive them on parkways?

How does an elephant get out of a small car?
The same way he got in.

How do you get five elephants into a small car?
Two in the back, two in front and one in the glove compartment.

How do you get a rhinoceros into a small car?
Chuck the elephants out.

Two big turtles and a small one went to have a root beer. It began to rain, and they decided that since the little turtle was fastest, he should go home for the umbrella.

The little turtle objected. He was afraid that if he left, the big turtles would drink his root beer. At last they convinced him they'd leave his root bear alone, and the little turtle set out for home.

Three weeks passed. Finally, one of the big turtles said, "I'm getting thirsty. Let's drink that little guy's root beer."

"I've been thinking the same thing." said the other.

From the other end of the room, a little voice cried, "Oh, no, you don't! If you do, I won't go home and get the umbrella!"

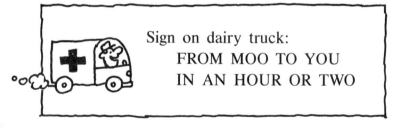

Sign on dairy truck:
FROM MOO TO YOU
IN AN HOUR OR TWO

What is the egg capital of the world?
New Yolk City.

What egg goes to faraway places?
An eggs-plorer.

What do you say to a hitchhiking frog?
"Hop in!"

What do you call an elephant hitchhiker?
A two-and-a-half ton pickup.

Why don't many elephants go to college?
Because so few graduate from high school.

Why are elephant rides cheaper than pony rides?
Because elephants work for peanuts.

Why don't elephants ride bicycles?
Because they have enough trouble riding their tricycles.

Where do people go dancing in California?
San Frandisco.

Some cowboys were talking about their horses.

One of them boasted, "I once owned the fastest horse in the state."

"How fast was that horse?" asked one of the listeners.

"That horse was so fast—well, just to give you an idea—I was riding him about 30 miles from home one day when a storm blew up. Well, that horse of mine raced the storm so close for those 30 miles that I didn't feel a drop of rain."

"Guess that's pretty fast," said one of his friends.

"Guess so!" said the cowboy. "My dog, who was only ten feet behind me, had to swim the whole way home!"

What goes, "Cluck, cluck, cluck, BOOM!"?
A chicken in a minefield.

ONE OF THE WORLD'S WORST
SHAGGY CHICKEN JOKES

Driving along a country road, a man noticed a chicken running alongside his car. The man increased his speed to 40 m.p.h. The chicken kept coming. The man stepped on the gas, but the chicken kept up. When the car reached 55 m.p.h., the chicken passed him and turned down a country road. It was then that the man saw that the chicken had three legs.

He followed the chicken to a farm. The barnyard was filled with three-legged chickens.

"Say," said the man to a farmer standing nearby, "do all your chickens have three legs?"

"Yes," replied the farmer.

"How do they taste?"

"Don't know," answered the farmer. "Haven't been able to catch one yet."

Why did the chicken run?
It saw the fox trot.

Why did the rabbit go to the barber?
To get a hare-cut.

Which traffic light is the bravest?
The one that doesn't turn yellow.

What country does candy come from?
Sweetzerland.

What takes an elephant up and down tall buildings?
An elephator (elevator).

What do you get if you cross an elephant and a water hose?
A jumbo jet.

What did the zookeeper say when he saw four elephants in sunglasses coming over a hill?
Nothing. He didn't recognize them.

9.
MOTHER
NATURE
STRIKES BACK

What did the rake say to the hoe?
"Hi, hoe!"

What has two tails, six feet and three trunks?
An elephant with spare parts.

Mama Skunk had two children and a very hard time keeping track of them. They were named In and Out. Whenever In was in, Out was out. And if Out was in, In was out.

One day she called Out and told him to bring In in. Out went right out and brought In back with him.

"Good!" said Mama Skunk. "But how in the great forest did you find him in such a short time?"

"It was easy," said Out. "In-stinct."

What gives milk, goes "moo" and makes all your wishes come true?
Your dairy godmother.

How do you move cows?
In a moo-ving van.

Why did the cow cross the road?
To see its fodder (father).

Which three states have the most cows?
Cow-lorado, Moo-souri and Cow-lifornia.

What cow do you sit on?
A cow-ch.

What do you get when you cross a rooster and a steer?

A cock-and-bull story.

What do you get when you cross a rooster and a duck?

A bird that wakes you at the quack of dawn.

What does a frog say when it sees something great?

"Toadly awesome!"

What is the difference between a coyote and a flea?

One howls on the prairie, the other prowls on the hairy.

What eats cheese and buzzes?

A mouse-quito.

What has six legs, bites and talks in code?

A morse-quito.

What do you call an insect from outer space?

Bug Rogers.

Why couldn't the butterfly go to the dance?

Because it was a moth ball.

What kind of shoes do toads wear?
Open toad shoes.

Which toad was a famous cowboy?
Buffalo Bill Toady.

What do you call a cowardly frog?
A chicken croak-ette.

WORLD'S BEST
TALKING-FROG JOKES

What does a frog with long ears say?
"Rabbit! Rabbit!"

What does a bandit frog say?
"Rob it! Rob it!"

What does a mechanical frog say?
"Robot! Robot!"

What does a frog welder say?
"Rivet! Rivet!"

What does a frog tailor say?
"Rip it! Rip it!"

What do you call a funny chicken?

A comedi-hen (comedienne).

What did the chick say when it came out of the shell?

"What an eggs-perience!"

What order did the bird general give to his army?

"We-tweet!"

Why do ducks have webbed feet?

To stamp out forest fires.

Why do elephants have flat feet?

To stamp out burning ducks.

Why are elephants wrinkled all over?

Because they're too big to put on an ironing board.

Why does a polar bear wear fur?
It would look silly in a vinyl raincoat.

What are spider's webs good for?
Spiders.

What do they call the carrot who talked back to
the farmer?
A fresh vegetable.

Did you hear the joke about the hot potato?
Never mind. Let's just drop it.

Which side of an apple is the reddest?
The outside.

Why did the lettuce close its eyes?
So it wouldn't see the salad dressing.

A diner in a restaurant called the waitress to his table. Pointing to a sad-looking baked potato on his plate, he said, "That potato is bad."

The waitress picked up the potato and slapped it roughly a couple of times. Then she put it back on the diner's plate.

"Now," she told the customer, "If that potato gives you any more trouble, you just let me know."

VEGETABLE LOVE STORY

Do you *carrot* all for me?
You are my *currant* love.
My heart *beets* for you.
I'm *melon-choly* all the *thyme* when I don't
    see you.
With your *turnip* nose, your *radish* hair and
    your *cherry* smile,
You're a real *peach*.
My *celery* may be tiny,
But *weed* make such a swell *pear*,
If we *cantaloupe*, *lettuce* marry soon.
No *sage* would interfere.

Who makes suits and eats spinach?
Popeye the Tailorman.

What is Tibetan, hairy and courageous?
Yak, the Giant Killer.

What is black and white and green and brown?
A zebra with a runny nose in a muddy field.

What is red then yellow, red then yellow?
A cherry that works part time as a banana.

What is purple, big and has an English accent?
Grape Britain.

What song do volcanoes sing?
"Lava, Come Back to Me."

What did the coal sing to the oil?
"What kind of fuel am I . . .?"

Did you hear the joke about the swan song?
Never mind. That's swan on you!

10. MONSTER MISFITS

How do Martians shave?
With laser blades.

What did the metric Martian say?
"Take me to your litre."

What did the boy say when the extraterrestrial went home?
"E.T. come, E.T. go."

What does E.T. stand for?
E.T. stands when he doesn't want to sit down.

Why does E.T. have such big eyes?
Because he saw his phone bill.

What happened to the monster who ate the electric company?
He went into shock.

Did you hear about the ghoul who sent his girl a heart for Valentine's Day— still beating?

What did the monster say when it saw Santa Clause?

"Yum, yum!"

What are the most popular stories among baby monsters?

"Little Boo Creep" and "Moldy Locks."

YOUNG MONSTER: Mother, will I ever be able to join the Army?

MOTHER MONSTER: No, but you can join the Ghost Guard.

What do little vampires need for all their toys?

Bat-teries.

What is a vampire's favorite athlete?

An acro-bat.

Why do vampires drink blood?

Root beer makes them burp.

Where does Count Dracula get his jokes?

From his crypt writer.

Did you hear about the new Dracula Doll? You put in a battery and it bites a Barbie Doll in the neck.

How do ghouls like their potatoes?
French fright.

What is a little ghoul's favorite game?
Corpse and Robbers.

What is nine feet tall and flies a kite in a rainstorm?
Benjamin Franklinstein.

What do you call the team of Frankenstein monsters who play football?
The All-Scars.

BOY FRANKENSTEIN: What lovely green eyes you have!
GIRL FRANKENSTEIN: Thank you! They were a birthday present.

What do you say before you start a meeting with ghosts?
"Please be sheeted."

What has a lot of teeth and goes, "Zip, zip, zip"?
A zipper.

Where do you find giant snails?
At the end of giants' fingers.

"Don't eat with your fingers, dear," said the giant to her son. "Use the shovel."

What has webbed feet and fangs?
Count Quackula.

Why aren't vampires welcome in blood banks?
Because they only want to make withdrawals.

Where in the navy would you find a vampire?
On a bat-tleship.

How many vampires does it take to change a light bulb?
None. Vampires prefer the dark.

What do you give a witch for her birthday?
A charm bracelet.

How did the two witches meet?
By chants.

INDEX